Ages 4 & 5

rainbowpublishers®

Rainbow Publishers • P.O. Box 261129 • San Diego, CA 92196
www.RainbowPublishers.com

FAVORITE
BIBLE FAMILIES

Ages 4 & 5

Bonnie Line

To Scott Howard and Nicholas: May Jesus be the love of your lives! Love, Grandma

FAVORITE BIBLE FAMILIES FOR AGES 4 & 5
©2010 by Rainbow Publishers
ISBN 10: 1-58411-023-6
ISBN 13: 978-1-58411-023-1
Rainbow reorder# RB38052
RELIGION / Christian Ministry / Children

Rainbow Publishers
P.O. Box 261129
San Diego, CA 92196
www.RainbowPublishers.com

Cover Illustrator: Court Patton
Interior Illustrator: Ron Forkner

Certified Chain of Custody
Promoting Sustainable
Forest Management
www.sfiprogram.org

SUSTAINABLE
FORESTRY
INITIATIVE

Scriptures are from the *Holy Bible: New International Version* (North American Edition), ©1973, 1978, 1984 by the International Bible Society. Used by permission of Zondervan Bible Publishers.

Printed in the United States of America

Contents

Introduction

We are all a part of some family, whether it is a family with parents and children, a family with a spouse, a larger extended family or God's family of believers. In the Bible, there were many different types of families. Some obeyed God, while others did not. Yet they are all important because we can learn from them how to live as a family and as Christians.

God has a purpose for each family. As a teacher, you have the awesome responsibility of introducing your students to how God uses families in the Bible and in today's lives. Four- and five-year-olds are just becoming aware of relationships within their own family. The activities in *Favorite Bible Families for Ages 4&5* are designed for identifying roles in families, explaining God's plan for families and instructing children about the consequences of obeying and disobeying God.

Each Bible family in this book is a lesson unit, with several themes that apply to the families. Suggestions for directed conversations with your children are contained in the "What to Say" section of each lesson. A materials list and step-by-step instructions will help you make the most of your lesson time. To minimize material costs, send home the reproducible Note to Families on page 9.

In the last chapter of the book, there are lessons for the Family of God. These four lessons explain the steps to receive Christ as Savior; it is never too early for kids to learn about God's salvation plan. And other family members may read the take-home lesson page and learn how they too can be a part of God's family!

TO FAMILIES OF FOUR- AND FIVE-YEAR-OLDS

We have some exciting activities planned for use in teaching Bible lessons this year. Some of these crafts use ordinary household items. We would like your help in saving these items for our activities.

❏ clear, self-stick plastic

❏ cotton balls

❏ craft sticks, 6" size

❏ dry, uncooked corn kernels

❏ gold ribbon, ¼"

❏ magazines

❏ paper cups

❏ paper grocery bags

❏ paper plates, large and dessert size

❏ paper towel rolls

❏ ribbon, ¼"

❏ safety pins

❏ string

❏ wild rice

❏ yarn

Please bring the items on _____.

Thank you for your help!

_____
Teacher

TO FAMILIES OF FOUR- AND FIVE-YEAR-OLDS

We have some exciting activities planned for use in teaching Bible lessons this year. Some of these crafts use ordinary household items. We would like your help in saving these items for our activities.

❏ clear, self-stick plastic

❏ cotton balls

❏ craft sticks, 6" size

❏ dry, uncooked corn kernels

❏ gold ribbon, ¼"

❏ magazines

❏ paper cups

❏ paper grocery bags

❏ paper plates, large and dessert size

❏ paper towel rolls

❏ ribbon, ¼"

❏ safety pins

❏ string

❏ wild rice

❏ yarn

Please bring the items on _____.

Thank you for your help!

_____
Teacher

Memory Verse Index

Adam and Eve's Family
Made by God

Memory Verse

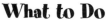

God created man in his own image.
~ Genesis 1:27

 what to say

God made the whole world. One day, God decided to create a man. He formed the man from the dirt of the earth. He breathed air into the man's lungs so the man could live. Then God created a woman so that the man wouldn't be alone. She was to be the man's helper. God called the man Adam and the woman Eve. God liked what He had made.

What You Need

- ❑ this page, duplicated
- ❑ crayons
- ❑ scissors
- ❑ glue sticks

What to Do

1. Have the children color Adam and Eve.
2. Help the students cut out Adam and Eve and the hands.
3. Show how to glue Adam and Eve to the hands.
4. Say, **God created the first family. God created you.** Emphasize how special each child is and then say, **And God said** (use each child's name) **is good.**

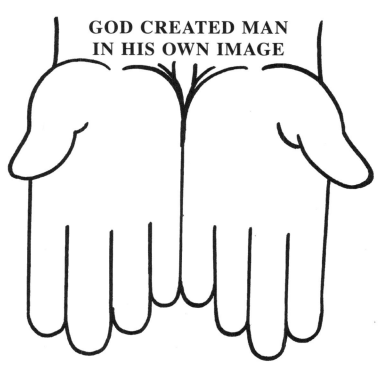

GOD CREATED MAN
IN HIS OWN IMAGE

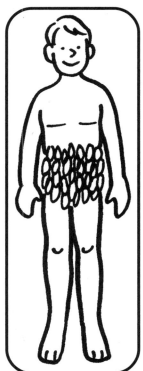

My Special Garden

Memory Verse

They will be yours for food.
~ Genesis 1:29

Before Class

Cut small pictures of plants, food, birds and animals from old magazines.

God made a special garden for Adam and Eve. There were big trees with fruit and nuts to eat. There were many plants with berries and vegetables to eat. Birds and animals also lived in this garden. God provided Adam and Eve with a beautiful place to live and good food to eat. It must have been fun to live in this special garden!

What You Need

☐ this page, duplicated
☐ old magazines
☐ crayons
☐ glue sticks

What to Do

1. Ask, **What kinds of flowers and trees would you plant in a garden? Would you have birds and animals living in it?**

2. Have the students select and glue pictures of plants, trees, birds and animals to the picture.

3. Instruct the children to draw happy faces on the kids in the picture.

4. Say, **God gives you good food to eat and a beautiful world with tall trees, blue skies and a big sun to keep you warm.**

Adam and Eve's Family
Closed Forever

Memory Verse

They hid from the Lord God.
~ Genesis 3:8

Before Class

Cut an 18" length of yarn for each child.

what to say

God made a special garden for Adam and Eve. They could eat from all of the trees except from the one in the middle of the garden. God told Adam he couldn't eat or even touch the fruit. One day, Adam and Eve ate from the tree. Then they heard God walking nearby and hid from Him. God loved Adam and Eve, but told them they could no longer live in His special garden because they had disobeyed Him.

What You Need

- ❏ this page, duplicated
- ❏ crayons
- ❏ scissors
- ❏ yarn
- ❏ hole punch

What to Do

1. Have the students color the sign.
2. Help the children cut out the sign and punch two holes at the top.
3. Instruct the students to thread the yarn through the holes, then tie the ends together for them.
4. Say, **God wants you to obey even when you don't want to.** Talk about how hard it is sometimes to obey, but emphasize that God is happy when we do.

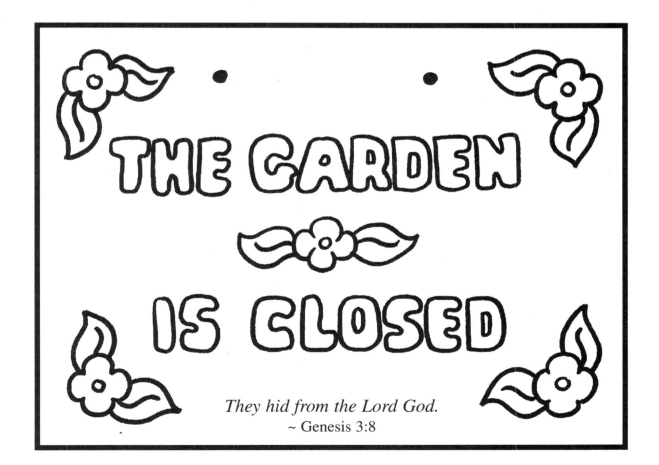

They hid from the Lord God.
~ Genesis 3:8

Adam and Eve's Family
Work and Play Together

Memory Verse

He created them male and female.
~ Genesis 5:2

what to say

Families are special. God created the very first family. Adam and Eve were the people He created. They lived in a special garden until they disobeyed God. After they left the garden, they had two sons. Their oldest son was named Cain and their youngest son was named Abel. They all worked hard to grow food to eat. Sometimes the boys got along and other times they didn't. But they were still God's first family.

What You Need

❏ this page, duplicated
❏ happy face stickers
❏ crayons

What to Do

1. Allow the students to stick a happy face on the pictures of children playing and working nicely.
2. Instruct them to draw a large X on the pictures of children being mean.
3. Say, **God wants you to be nice to others, especially your family.** Talk about how families are special.

Noah's Family
Making the Right Choices

Memory Verse

*Noah was a
righteous man.*
~ Genesis 6:9

what to say

God made two people to start the first family, but soon there were many people who lived on the earth. They did whatever they wanted. They didn't care about anything but making themselves happy. This made God angry. On the whole earth, there was only one man who loved and worshipped God. His name was Noah. He always tried to please God. This made God happy. He loved Noah because he was a righteous man.

What You Need

☐ this page, duplicated
☐ crayons

What to Do

1. Have the students connect the broken lines to find the answer to what they need to do each day.
2. Read the words to the class.
3. Instruct the students to draw a happy face inside the heart.
4. Say, **God is happy when you choose to do what pleases Him. You can please God by sharing your toys and obeying your parents and teachers.** Ask them how they feel when they please their parents.

Noah's Family
Two by Two Ark

Memory Verse

Noah did...as God commanded him.
~ Genesis 6:22

what to say

Noah was the only man who tried to please God. One day, God told Noah He was going to send a flood. Noah would need to build a big boat, called an ark. He was to bring two of each animal to live on the ark. So Noah began to build the ark. It took him a long time, but it had to be big enough to keep his family and the animals safe from the flood.

What You Need

❑ this page, duplicated
❑ crayons

What to Do

1. Instruct the students to draw a line to match the animals that are the same.
2. Say, **The ark had to carry enough food to feed Noah, his family and all the animals. How many animals do you think the ark could hold?**

18

Noah's Family
Waiting for the Raindrops

Bible Story

Noah's family and the animals go into the ark. (Gen. 6:1-22 & 7:1-5)

Memory Verse

The Lord then said to Noah, "Go into the ark."
~ Genesis 7:1

what to say

God told Noah there was going to be a flood. God helped Noah build a big boat called an ark. It took Noah a long time to build it. When the ark was finished, Noah brought his wife, his sons and their wives on to the ark to live. He also brought two of each animal. He brought enough food for all of the people and animals to eat. They all lived on the ark while they waited for the rain to start.

What You Need

☐ this page, duplicated
☐ crayons

What to Do

1. Have the children color the raindrops. As the children are coloring, talk about animals they have seen and what kinds of food they eat.
2. Ask, **How many raindrops are there?**
3. Say, **It rained for 40 days and nights. God watched over Noah and his family. God watches over you.**

Noah's Family
Safety First

Memory Verse

He...sent out the dove.
~ Genesis 8:10

Before Class

Cut one 6" length of yarn for each child.

what to say

It rained for 40 days and nights. Noah, his family and the animals were all safe in the ark Noah built. After the rain stopped, the land was still covered with water. Noah waited a while. Then he sent a dove out three times to find dry land. The second time, the dove returned with a twig from a tree. The third time, the dove found dry land and did not return to the ark. God used a dove to show Noah it was safe for everyone to leave the ark.

What You Need

- [ ] this page, duplicated
- [ ] glue sticks
- [ ] scissors
- [ ] cotton balls
- [ ] small twigs
- [ ] yarn
- [ ] hole punch

What to Do

1. Give each child two copies of the dove. Allow them to color the pictures.
2. Help the students cut out the two sides of the dove.
3. Show how to glue the dove together except for the very top.
4. Give the students some cotton balls to stuff into the dove. Then help them glue the top shut.
5. Give each student a small twig to glue to the dove's beak.
6. Punch a hole in each dove and tie a string through it.
7. Say, **You can hang the dove in your room at home.**

He...sent out the dove.
Genesis 8:10

Noah's Family
An Altar for God

Memory Verse

I have set my rainbow in the clouds.
~ Genesis 9:13

Before Class

Duplicate or trace the rocks on brown or gray paper.

what to say

When the land was dry, Noah, his family and the animals left the ark. Noah wanted to thank God for keeping them safe as He said He would. Noah built an altar to God. God was pleased. He promised Noah that He would never send another flood to destroy the earth. Then God gave Noah the sign of the rainbow to remind him of the promise. God always keeps His promises.

What You Need

- ❏ pages 21 and 22, duplicated
- ❏ brown or gray paper
- ❏ scissors
- ❏ crayons
- ❏ glue sticks

What to Do

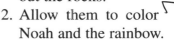

1. Have the students cut out the rocks.
2. Allow them to color Noah and the rainbow.
3. Instruct the students to glue the rocks on the altar.
4. Talk about what a promise is. Say, **Remember, God always keeps His promises.**

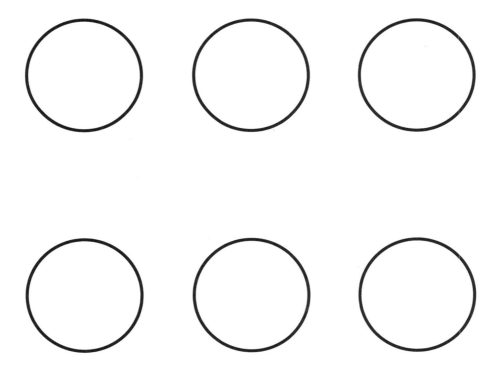

I have set my rainbow in the clouds.
Genesis 9:13

Abraham's Family
Traveling the Road with God

Memory Verse

Leave your country.
~ Genesis 12:1

what to say

God told Abram that He wanted him to leave his home. Abram had to leave all his friends. He took his wife and nephew and did as God told him. They traveled a long time until they finally got to their new country, called Canaan. It must have been difficult for Abram to leave, but he loved and trusted God. Because he obeyed, God blessed Abram and his family.

What You Need

- [ ] this page, duplicated
- [ ] pencils

What to Do

1. Have the students follow the dots to see Abram's new home.

2. As you help the children connect the dots, talk about what they would take on a long trip. Ask them if they have ever taken a vacation far from home.

3. Say, **It took Abram a long time to get to Canaan because he had to walk. We can travel a long way today by car and get there much faster. Abram was wise to follow God, even though it was difficult.**

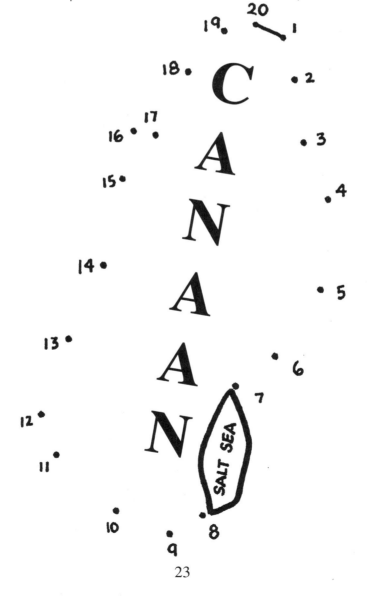

Abraham's Family
Too Many Sheep

Memory Verse

For we are brothers.
~ Genesis 13:8

what to say

Abram, his wife and his nephew Lot moved to a land called Canaan. They lived in tents with all their possessions. Abram and Lot had flocks and herds of animals. The land couldn't feed all of the animals, so the workers began fighting over the land. To keep the peace, Abram decided he and Lot would have to divide the land. Abram gave Lot the first choice of which land he wanted. Lot chose the land he thought was the best. God was pleased with Abram for keeping the peace.

What You Need

- ☐ this page, duplicated
- ☐ crayons
- ☐ glue sticks
- ☐ cotton balls

What to Do

1. Have the children color the picture of Abram and Lot.
2. Show how to glue cotton balls on the sheep.
3. Say, **There were so many sheep that there wasn't enough land to feed them all. God was pleased that Abram chose to keep the peace. You can please God when you let others go first.**

Abraham's Family
Count the Stars

Memory Verse

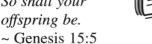

So shall your offspring be.
~ Genesis 15:5

 **what to say**

Abram loved, worshipped and obeyed God. He and his wife, Sarai, had no children. When Abram and Sarai died, their possessions would go to a servant. This made Abram sad. One day, God asked Abram what he wanted. Abram told God that he and Sarai wanted children, but they knew they were too old. God told Abram he would have a son. He told him that his relatives would be more than the stars in the sky.

What You Need

❑ this page, duplicated
❑ scissors
❑ colored star stickers
❑ crayons

What to Do

1. Have the students cut out the star.
2. Help the children print their names on their stars.
3. Allow the students to stick colored stars on it, one for each member of their family.
4. Ask, **Have you ever tried to count the stars at night? There are too many to count! When God told Abram He would give him more relatives than stars in the sky, He meant He would bless him a lot.** Talk about ways God blesses us with family, such as parents, brothers and sisters and extended family.

So shall your offspring be.
~ Genesis 15:5

Abraham's Family
New Names

Memory Verse

Your name will be Abraham.
~ Genesis 17:5

what to say

Abram and Sarai were old and had no children when God promised them a son would be born to them. God changed Abram's name to Abraham, which means "father of many."

God also changed Sarai's name to Sarah. He said that kings would come from her family. God blessed Abraham and Sarah. They would be the father and mother to many nations.

What You Need

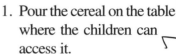

❑ this page, duplicated
❑ glue
❑ alphabet cereal

What to Do

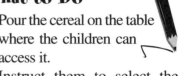

1. Pour the cereal on the table where the children can access it.
2. Instruct them to select the correct letter and glue several on the letters on their page. For example, they should glue A's on the "A" in Abraham, B's on the "B" and so on.
3. Say, **Your name tells others who you are. You are special to God.**

Abraham's Family
A Blanket for Isaac

Memory Verse

I have borne him a son.
~ Genesis 21:7

Before Class

Cut out pieces of flannel (2" x 1").

what to say

God promised Abraham and Sarah they would have a son. They knew they were too old to have children. Yet they also knew that God could do miracles. When Sarah gave birth to her son, Isaac, she knew God had kept His promise. Abraham and Sarah now had a family that would grow and some day live in every country on earth, just as God had said. God keeps His promises.

What You Need

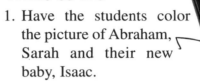

- ❏ this page, duplicated
- ❏ crayons
- ❏ glue sticks
- ❏ flannel

What to Do

1. Have the students color the picture of Abraham, Sarah and their new baby, Isaac.

2. Encourage the children to draw a smile on each of their faces.

3. Show how to glue a "blanket" (a piece of flannel) on Isaac to keep him warm.

4. Say, **Abraham and Sarah were happy when their son was born. Your parents were happy and smiled when they saw you for the first time after you were born, too.** Talk about how all children are special to their parents. Say, **God is happy when parents and children love each other.**

Isaac's Family
A Hairy Baby

Memory Verse

There were twin boys.
~ Genesis 25:24

Before Class

Unravel some brown yarn for the craft.

what to say

When Isaac was 40 years old, he married a woman named Rebekah. They wanted to have children. They tried for 20 years. Isaac prayed for God's help. Soon, Rebekah gave birth to twin boys. The first twin was named Esau. The second twin was named Jacob. Even though the boys were twins, they did not look alike. Esau was hairy, while Jacob wasn't. God answered Isaac's prayer when He gave him twin boys.

What You Need

- ❑ this page, duplicated
- ❑ 6" craft sticks
- ❑ glue sticks
- ❑ brown yarn
- ❑ scissors

What to Do

1. Help the students cut out the baby boys.
2. Show how to glue the bottom half of each baby to a craft stick.
3. Ask, **Can you tell which twin is Esau and which one is Jacob?**
4. Instruct the children to glue some unraveled yarn to look like hair onto the arms and legs of one baby.
5. Say, **Now can you tell which one is Esau?** Ask the students if they know of any identical twins. Emphasize that Isaac and Rebekah's twins were a special answer to prayer.

Isaac's Family
Food Swap

Memory Verse

So Esau despised his birthright.
~ Genesis 25:34

what to say

In Bible times, the first-born son of each family became the leader of the family when the father died. This son would receive the largest share of everything his father owned. Esau and Jacob were twins, but Esau was born first. He liked being outdoors. One day, he came home very hungry and asked Jacob for some food. Jacob told Esau he would give him some if he gave him the birthright. Without thinking, Esau said yes. Later, he was sorry he had made the swap.

What You Need

❑ this page, duplicated
❑ crayons

What to Do

1. Have the students color the picture of Esau trading his birthright to Jacob for a plate of food.
2. Say, **We often want something right away. But sometimes it is better to wait. Esau wanted the food right away. He made a bad choice by giving in to his selfish desires.**

Esau traded his birthright for a plate of food.

Isaac's Family
Look Alikes

Memory Verse

Your brother...took your blessing.
~ Genesis 27:35

what to say

Isaac was very old and couldn't see. He asked his oldest son, Esau, to prepare a special meal for him so he could give him the blessing. Esau left to go hunting. Jacob, his twin brother, wanted the blessing, so he put on Esau's clothes. Esau was hairy, so Jacob covered his hands and neck with goatskins. Jacob pretended to be Esau. Isaac gave him the blessing. When Esau heard, he was very angry at Jacob.

What You Need

❑ this page, duplicated
❑ crayons

What to Do

1. Have the students circle the twins that are the same. Say, **Look carefully to make sure they are the same!**
2. Say, **You are special to God. You don't need to pretend to be someone else.** Talk about how pretending to be someone else is wrong. Give examples, such as pretending to have a birthday just to get gifts or pretending to be sick to get attention.

Isaac's Family
Promise Rock

Memory Verse

This stone...will be God's house.
~ Genesis 28:22

Before Class

Use the pattern below to trace and cut out two rocks from brown paper for each child. Write "Promise Rock" in the centers of the rocks.

what to say

Esau and Jacob were twin brothers, but they didn't always get along. Jacob took the birthright and blessing that belonged to Esau. Esau became so angry that Jacob ran away in fear for his life. After walking all day, he stopped to rest and fell asleep. In a dream, God told him He would watch over him and that many good things would come to him. In the morning, Jacob promised God that if He would watch over him, he would follow Him.

What You Need

- ❏ this page, duplicated
- ❏ scissors
- ❏ tissue paper
- ❏ glue sticks
- ❏ brown paper

What to Do

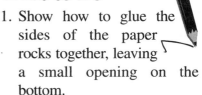

1. Show how to glue the sides of the paper rocks together, leaving a small opening on the bottom.
2. Help the students carefully stuff tissue paper into the opening and glue it shut.
3. Say, **Just as God promised He would watch over Jacob, God watches over you.** Talk about how God watches over them even when they do bad things.

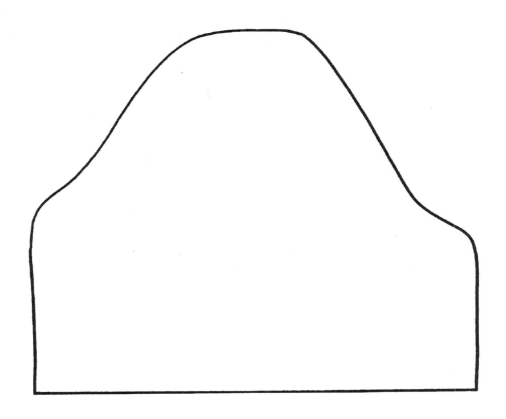

Isaac's Family
Family Photo Album

Memory Verse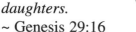

Laban had two daughters.
~ Genesis 29:16

Before Class

Bring a photo album to class so you can share your family photos with the children.

what to say

Jacob went to live with his Uncle Laban, who had two daughters. Jacob worked hard each day. When Laban asked him what he wanted for payment, Jacob told him he wanted to marry his youngest daughter, Rachel. Laban fooled him and gave him his oldest daughter, Leah, instead. Jacob was mad. Laban agreed to give his youngest daughter if Jacob worked longer. Jacob agreed. God watched over Jacob and blessed him with a large family.

What You Need

- ❏ page 33, duplicated
- ❏ white paper
- ❏ crayons
- ❏ stapler
- ❏ tape

What to Do

1. Give the children paper to draw pictures of their family.
2. Instruct the students to color the photo album cover.
3. Go around and staple each album together with the cover on top and a blank sheet of paper in back. Cover each staple with tape to avoid injury.
4. Say, **You can share your family photo album and tell others that God watches over your family.**

MY FAMILY PHOTO ALBUM

Isaac's Family
Love Bears All Maze

Memory Verse

And they wept.
~ Genesis 33:4

what to say

For many years, Jacob lived far from home. He married, had children and owned servants and flocks. One day, God spoke to Jacob and told him it was time to go home. Jacob and his family, along with his servants and animals, began the long trip home. When he was almost there, Jacob sent servants ahead to tell Esau, his brother, he was coming. He was afraid Esau might still be mad. Instead, Esau hugged and kissed Jacob. He had forgiven Jacob.

What You Need

- ❑ this page, duplicated
- ❑ crayons
- ❑ heart stickers

What to Do

1. Instruct the students to draw a line on the path Jacob took when he returned home.
2. Allow the students to color the picture of the brothers and stick hearts by Jacob and Esau.
3. Say, **God watched over Jacob while he was away from his home.** Explain how love helps us forgive others.

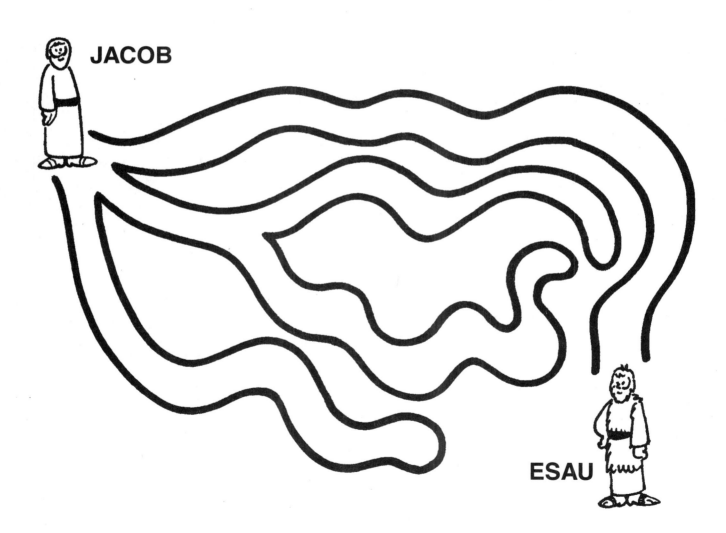

JACOB

ESAU

Joseph's Family
Robe of Many Colors

Memory Verse

He made a...robe for him.
~ Genesis 37:3

Before Class

Tear colored paper into medium-sized pieces and cut the paper bags as shown below to make a robe for each child.

Joseph was one of 12 brothers who helped take care of the sheep his family owned. When Joseph was 17, his father made a special robe for him. It had many colors. One day his brothers, who were jealous of him, sold Joseph to some people traveling nearby. These people took him to Egypt and sold him as a slave. Joseph was very far from home, but he trusted God to take care of him.

What You Need

❑ paper grocery bags
❑ scissors
❑ colored paper
❑ glue sticks

What to Do

1. Have the students glue pieces of colored paper on their robes.
2. Say, **When you are finished, you can pretend you are Joseph wearing his beautiful robe of many colors. As God watched over Joseph and took care of him, God will watch over and take care of you!**

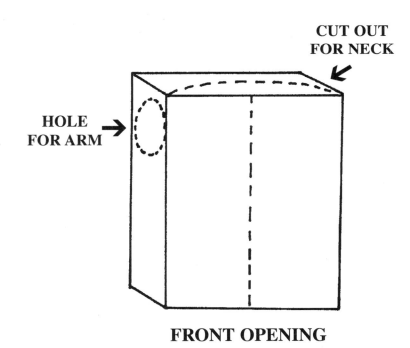

CUT OUT
FOR NECK

HOLE
FOR ARM

FRONT OPENING

35

Joseph's Family
Jailed Because of a Lie

Memory Verse

The Lord was with Joseph.
~ Genesis 39:2

what to say

Joseph was sold by his brothers. He became a slave to an Egyptian man named Potiphar. Potiphar was a guard for Pharaoh, the king of Egypt. Everything that Joseph did, God blessed. Potiphar knew Joseph's God was pleased with Joseph. One day, Potiphar's wife wanted Joseph to do something bad. Joseph said no because it would not please God. She told a lie and said he had done it, so Joseph was put in jail. Joseph still trusted God.

What You Need

- [ ] this page, duplicated
- [ ] crayons
- [ ] glue sticks
- [ ] chenille wires (4" long)

What to Do

1. Have the students color the picture of Joseph in prison.

2. Show how to glue the chenille wires for bars on the prison door.

3. Instruct them to draw a smile on Joseph because he still trusted God.

4. Ask the students if they have ever lied and what happened when they did. Say, **Joseph honored God by doing what was right. When you tell a lie, God is unhappy with you. But you can tell God you are sorry and He will forgive you.**

Joseph's Family
I Work for God Hat

Memory Verse

The Lord...gave him success.
~ Genesis 39:23

Before Class

Duplicate and cut out two of the hat pattern for each child.

what to say

While Joseph was in jail, he still trusted God. The king's baker and cupbearer were also in jail. They each had a dream they didn't understand. Joseph helped explain their dreams to them. They were happy and promised to help Joseph when they got out of prison. Once they got out, they forgot their promise. God continued to watch over Joseph while he was in jail.

What You Need

- ❑ page 38, duplicated
- ❑ scissors
- ❑ crayons
- ❑ glue sticks

What to Do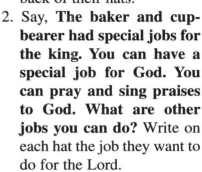

1. Allow the students to color the front and back of their hats.
2. Say, **The baker and cupbearer had special jobs for the king. You can have a special job for God. You can pray and sing praises to God. What are other jobs you can do?** Write on each hat the job they want to do for the Lord.
3. Help the students glue their hats together. Allow to dry.

Joseph's Family
Happy Face Cup

Memory Verse

You shall be in charge.
~ Genesis 41:40

Before Class

Poke holes in the bottoms of the cups ahead of time.

what to say

Joseph was in jail when Pharaoh, the king of Egypt, had two dreams. Pharaoh heard Joseph could explain dreams. Pharaoh asked Joseph to explain what his dreams meant. Joseph told Pharaoh God gave him the dreams because a famine would start soon. Pharaoh was so happy with Joseph for telling him about his dream that he let Joseph out of jail and made him a very important helper. Everyone had to obey everything Joseph said. God continued to watch over Joseph.

What You Need

- ❑ white paper cups
- ❑ 6" craft sticks
- ❑ glue sticks

What to Do

1. Have the students color the smiling face and heart.

2. Help them cut out both pieces, then glue the face on a paper cup turned upside-down.

3. Instruct the children to glue the heart on the top end of a craft stick and push the stick through the hole in the bottom of the cup. Only the heart will show.

4. Say, **The smiling face is you and the heart is God. You can be happy because God watches over you day and night!** Ask them how they feel because God watches over them all the time.

You shall be in charge.
Genesis 41:40

Joseph's Family
Saving for the Famine

Memory Verse

The seven years of famine began.
~ Genesis 41:54

what to say

Joseph lived in Egypt. He was 30 years old when Pharaoh put him in charge of the people. God showed Pharaoh in a dream that a famine was coming. A famine is when there isn't enough food to eat. The famine would last seven years. Joseph showed the Egyptians how to save some of their food. When the famine began, other countries didn't have enough food. Only Egypt had enough food because the people had listened to Joseph. Joseph got his wisdom from God.

What You Need

- ☐ this page, duplicated
- ☐ glue
- ☐ crayons
- ☐ unpopped popcorn

What to Do

1. Have the students color the picture of people saving grain for their storehouses.

2. Instruct them to glue two kernels of corn on the outstretched hand of the person who isn't holding a basket.

3. Say, **The Egyptians learned how to save their crops, so when the famine began, they had food.** Ask them how they feel when they are hungry and when they are full. Tell them they should say thank You to God for food. Say, **God watched over Joseph, just like He watches over you.**

Joseph's Family
Forgiving Others

Memory Verse

I am Joseph!
~ Genesis 45:3

Before Class

Use the pattern below to trace and cut out a heart from red paper for each child. Write "I forgive others because God forgives me" on each one. Cut each one in half.

what to say

God prepared Egypt for the coming famine. The other countries didn't know about the famine and didn't save extra food. Joseph's brothers came to Egypt because they had heard they could buy food there. At first, they didn't recognize Joseph. When Joseph saw his brothers, who had sold him as a slave, he forgave them and gave them food. Joseph had been through some terrible times, but this was all God's plan. Joseph was able to help his family have food during the famine.

What You Need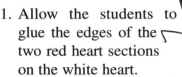

- [ ] this page, duplicated
- [ ] glue sticks
- [ ] red construction paper

What to Do

1. Allow the students to glue the edges of the two red heart sections on the white heart.
2. Say, **When you are mad at someone, remember Joseph. He forgave his brothers. God also forgives us.** Ask, **Is there anyone you need to forgive today?**

Moses' Family
Hiding in the Grass

Memory Verse

She named him Moses.
~ Exodus 2:10

Before Class

Fringe small strips of green paper to represent grass.

what to say

God's people lived as slaves in Egypt. Pharaoh, the king of Egypt, didn't like them. He said none of the baby boys could live. Moses was just a baby. His mother made a basket and put him in it. She put the basket in the Nile River grass. His sister, Miriam, watched to see what would happen. Pharaoh's daughter was bathing in the Nile and saw the basket. She took Moses home with her.

What You Need

- [ ] this page, duplicated
- [ ] glue sticks
- [ ] crayons
- [ ] green paper

What to Do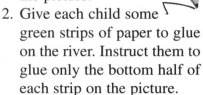

1. Have the children color the picture.
2. Give each child some green strips of paper to glue on the river. Instruct them to glue only the bottom half of each strip on the picture.
3. Say, **The green strips are the grass that hid Moses while he floated down the river. God watched over Moses. God watches over you all the time.**

Moses' Family
Who Sees Me Puzzle

Memory Verse

Then Moses was afraid.
~ Exodus 2:14

what to say

Moses was one of God's people who lived in Egypt. When he was a baby, his mother put him in a basket on the Nile River. Pharaoh's daughter found him and raised him as her own son. When Moses was a young man, he saw an Egyptian man hitting one of God's people. Moses thought no one was looking, so he killed the Egyptian. Someone did see him. When Pharaoh found out, he wanted to kill Moses, so Moses ran away.

What You Need

- ❑ this page, duplicated
- ❑ crayons

What to Do

1. Have the students color each part of the puzzle with the correct color.

2. When they are finished, there will be three places they didn't color. Help the students write each letter on the lines below the puzzle.

3. Say, **God sees everything you do. He loves you and forgives you even when you do bad things.** Ask the students if they have ever done something bad and how they felt when they asked God to forgive them. Emphasize that God loves them and always forgives them.

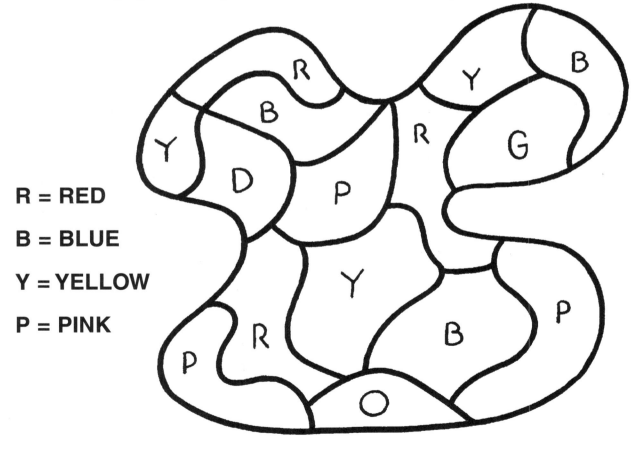

R = RED

B = BLUE

Y = YELLOW

P = PINK

Do You Hear What I Hear?

Memory Verse

Moses said, "Here I am."

~ Exodus 3:4

what to say

Moses killed an Egyptian. He ran far away because Pharaoh was angry with him. When he came to a well, he helped some young women give water to their sheep. They told their father what happened. He invited Moses to live with them.

Moses married one of the man's daughters. One day, Moses saw a burning bush. When he got closer, he heard God call his name: "Moses!" He answered God, saying, "Here I am."

What You Need

- ☐ this page, duplicated
- ☐ 12" chenille wire
- ☐ stapler
- ☐ scissors
- ☐ tape

What to Do

1. Have the students cut out the two Bibles.
2. Help the children staple the Bibles to chenille wires and fit them around their ears. They should put a piece of tape on the staples to avoid injury.
3. Say, **God's voice is the message in the Bible. Your teacher, mom or dad can read you God's words so you can hear His voice.**

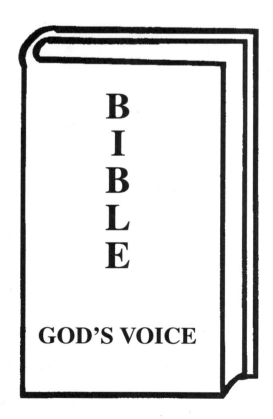

Moses' Family
Staff or Snake Twister

Memory Verse

I will help you speak.
~ Exodus 4:12

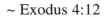 **what to say**

God spoke to Moses through a burning bush and told him to go back to Egypt. God wanted Moses to lead His people out of Egypt to a new land. Moses complained to God that he didn't know how to speak properly. He was afraid that the people would not listen to him. God gave Moses a staff that became a snake when it was thrown on the ground to prove Moses was speaking God's words. God promised to help Moses. Moses obeyed God.

What You Need

- ❏ this page, duplicated
- ❏ 6" craft sticks
- ❏ scissors
- ❏ crayons
- ❏ glue sticks

What to Do

1. Have the students color the staff and the snake.
2. Instruct them to cut out both pieces. They should glue the staff on one side of a craft stick and the snake on the other side.
3. When the glue has dried, show how to place the stick between your hands and turn the stick back and forth.
4. Say, **Moses had a staff and then a snake. God helps us when we obey Him.** Emphasize that God helps us to tell the truth.

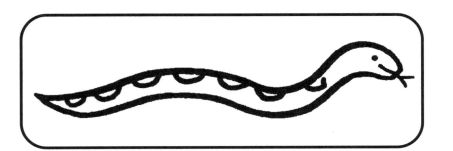

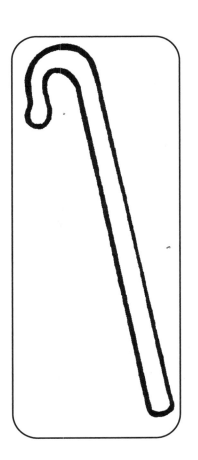

No, You Can't Go

Memory Verse

Let my people go.
~ Exodus 8:1

what to say

God told Moses to lead His people to a new land. God let Moses take his brother Aaron with him. God said He would teach them what to say. Moses and Aaron went to Pharaoh, the king of Egypt, and told him to let God's people go. Each time Pharaoh said no, God sent a plague. God sent plagues of blood, livestock, frogs, gnats, flies, boils, hail, locusts and darkness. Pharaoh still would not let God's people go with Moses and Aaron.

What You Need

❑ this page, duplicated
❑ crayons

What to Do

1. Have the students color the picture.
2. Say, **Each time Pharaoh said no, God sent a plague.**
3. Instruct the students to draw sad faces on Moses and Aaron.
4. Talk about how they feel when they ask for something and the person says no. Ask how they feel when the person says yes. Say, **God was not happy that Pharaoh was saying no to His people.**

Moses' Family
Sand Under My Feet

Memory Verse

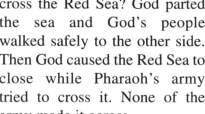

Do not be afraid.
Stand firm.
~ Exodus 14:13

what to say

After God sent many plagues on Egypt, Pharaoh let God's people go. Moses, Aaron and all the people walked through the desert until they came to the Red Sea. When they looked back, they saw Pharaoh's army chasing them. How would they cross the Red Sea? God parted the sea and God's people walked safely to the other side. Then God caused the Red Sea to close while Pharaoh's army tried to cross it. None of the army made it across.

What You Need

- ❑ this page, duplicated
- ❑ crayons
- ❑ glue sticks
- ❑ sandpaper

What to Do

1. Have the students color the feet.
2. Help them to carefully put glue on the bottom of the feet and place sandpaper on the glue.
3. Say, **God took care of His people and let them walk on dry sand to cross the Red Sea. When you need help, ask God. He will take care of you.**

Do not be afraid.

Stand firm.
~ Exodus 14:13

Moses' Family
Blue Ribbon Rules

Memory Verse

I will write on them the words.
~ Exodus 34:1

what to say

It had been three months since the Israelites left Egypt. They camped in the desert near the base of a mountain. Moses and Aaron climbed the mountain to spend quiet time with God. After some time, Aaron came down the mountain. Moses stayed to write on stone tablets the rules that God had given him. He was gone so long that the people thought he had died. When Moses came down the mountain, the people were doing bad things. In anger, Moses broke the stone tablets.

What You Need

- ❏ this page, duplicated
- ❏ crayons
- ❏ small, blue ribbon stickers

What to Do

1. Have the students circle the pictures of children doing good things.
2. Instruct the students to put a blue ribbon sticker by each picture that shows something they do at their house.
3. Say, **God wants us to live together and help each other. You can help at home by putting your toys away.** Ask what rules they have to follow at Sunday school and at home. Ask why they think it is important to have rules.

Moses' Family
Glittering Water

Memory Verse

Speak to that rock before their eyes.
~ Numbers 20:8

Before Class

Cut small pieces of aluminum foil. Shape a chenille wire into a staff for each child.

 **what to say**

The Israelites wandered in the desert for many years. God provided what they needed, but the people were not easy to please. They complained because there was no water. God told Moses and Aaron to speak to a certain rock and water would come out of it. Because he was angry with the people for complaining, Moses struck the rock with his staff instead of talking to it as God had instructed. God then became angry with Moses and told him he couldn't live in the Promised Land.

What You Need

- ☐ this page, duplicated
- ☐ crayons
- ☐ 3" brown chenille wire
- ☐ aluminum foil
- ☐ glue sticks

What to Do

1. Have the students glue the chenille wire staff to Moses' hand.
2. Instruct the students to glue a piece of aluminum foil on the rock to look like water.
3. Say, **Moses didn't obey God. You can obey God and make Him happy. What rules do we need to obey?**

Ruth's Family
A Heart of Love

Memory Verse

Where you go I will go.
~ Ruth 1:16

what to say

Naomi had a husband named Elimelech and two sons. Elimelech moved the family to another country, called Moab. Then Elimelech died. Naomi's two sons married women from Moab. Then the two sons died, too. Now Naomi had no husband or sons to take care of her. She decided to return to her homeland to find a relative to help her. Ruth, one of her daughters-in-law, loved Naomi. She went with her to watch over her.

What You Need
- [ ] this page, duplicated
- [ ] glue
- [ ] circle-shaped cereal

What to Do

1. Have the students carefully draw a line of glue on the heart shape.
2. Give the students cereal to press into the glue. (Bring extra for snacking.)
3. Say, **Ruth loved Naomi enough to travel to a new country. God loves you. He goes with you each day as you play outside or visit a friend. Share how you show love to your family.**

GOD LOVES ME!

Ruth's Family
Find the Hidden Food

Memory Verse

*May the Lord
repay you.*
~ Ruth 2:12

what to say

Naomi and Ruth traveled back to Judah where Naomi had relatives. Both Naomi and Ruth's husbands had died. Ruth wanted to take care of Naomi, her husband's mother. Ruth collected the grain the workers missed when they picked the fields. Boaz owned the fields. He was Naomi's relative. Boaz heard how Ruth showed love and kindness to Naomi. Boaz let Ruth work in his fields so she and Naomi would have food to eat. God watched over Naomi and Ruth.

What You Need

- ❑ this page, duplicated
- ❑ crayons

What to Do

1. Have the students find the food that is hidden in the picture.
2. Ask, **Which food is your favorite? Ruth showed love to Naomi by finding food they could eat. You can show love by helping your mom or dad fix dinner.**

Ruth's Family
Picture Perfect

Memory Verse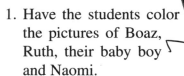

She became his wife.
~ Ruth 4:13

what to say

Naomi knew God wanted Ruth to get married again and have children. She told Ruth to find favor with Boaz, a relative of Naomi's. Naomi also told her to let Boaz know she was ready to get married. Boaz knew it would please God if he married Ruth. Later, after they got married, Ruth had a baby boy. Naomi was happy because Ruth trusted God. God took care of Naomi and Ruth.

What You Need

- ❏ this page, duplicated
- ❏ crayons
- ❏ glue
- ❏ craft sticks

What to Do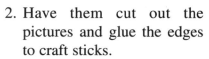

1. Have the students color the pictures of Boaz, Ruth, their baby boy and Naomi.
2. Have them cut out the pictures and glue the edges to craft sticks.
3. Encourage the children to take turns telling the Bible story to each other with the puppets.
4. Say, **God knows what is best for us. You can trust God to give you His very best.**

Hannah's Family
Sponge Letter Spelling

Memory Verse

I asked the Lord for him.
~ 1 Samuel 1:20

Before Class

Trace the letters below to make patterns, then trace them on thin sponges and cut them out. Make one set for every 3-4 children.

what to say

Hannah was married to a man named Elkanah. They were married for many years but they had no children. Hannah trusted God. One time while she was at the temple praying, Eli, the priest, saw her and went to talk to her. Hannah told Eli she was praying to God for a baby. Eli told her to go in peace. God answered Hannah's prayer. She gave birth to a baby boy.

What You Need

- ❑ this page, duplicated
- ❑ thin sponges
- ❑ white paper
- ❑ water-based paint
- ❑ paint smocks

What to Do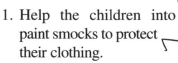

1. Help the children into paint smocks to protect their clothing.
2. Give each child a sheet of paper.
3. Help the students sponge paint the words below.
4. Say, **Hannah was thankful when God answered her prayer to have a baby. You can be thankful to God for parents, food, clothes and toys.** Share with your students some answers you have had to your prayers.

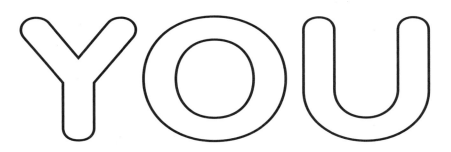

Hannah's Family
A Robe with a Heart

Memory Verse

Now I give him to the Lord.
~ 1 Samuel 1:28

Before Class

Trace the robe on brown paper and the heart on red paper for each child.

what to say

Hannah made a special promise to God. She said if God would give her a son, she would give her son to the Lord to serve Him. God gave her a son named Samuel. When Samuel was only 3 years old, Hannah took him to Eli, the priest, to live at the temple. Eli raised Samuel to love and worship God. Each year, Hannah brought Samuel a new coat. It must have been difficult for Hannah to leave her son, but she trusted God. Hannah kept her promise to God.

What You Need

- ❏ this page, duplicated
- ❏ glue sticks
- ❏ scissors
- ❏ brown and red construction paper

What to Do

1. Help the students cut out the robe and heart on the solid lines.
2. Show how to fold the robe and glue the heart on the inside.
3. Say, **Samuel learned about God from Eli the priest. You can know about God by listening to Bible stories.** Explain how listening to the Bible and memorizing Scripture can help them know God.

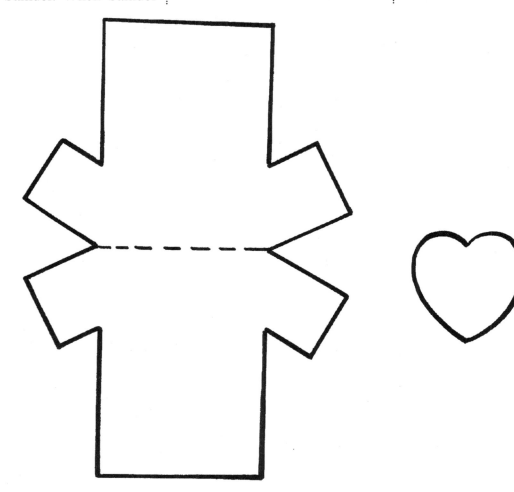

54

Hannah's Family
Joyful Letters

Memory Verse

My heart rejoices in the Lord.
~ 1 Samuel 2:1

what to say

It's easy to be happy when you have everything you want. But when you want something, it can be hard to wait for it. Hannah wanted a son but it took many years of praying before God answered her.

When she had a son, she was so happy, she wanted to say thank You to God. So she began to praise Him. Hannah was happy and full of God's joy.

What You Need

❑ this page, duplicated
❑ crayons

What to Do

1. Have the students only print the letters on the lines that have a heart above them.
2. Have the students read the words from the letters (GOD GIVES ME JOY).
3. Talk about how happy the students are when they receive presents. Tell them that God gave us a special present, Jesus. Say, **He gives us joy!**

___ ___ ___ ___ ___ ___ ___ ___ ___ ___ ___ ___ .

Hannah's Family
Blessings from God

Memory Verse

The Lord was gracious to Hannah.
~ 1 Samuel 2:21

what to say

Hannah loved the Lord. She trusted Him with all of her problems. After many years of praying, she finally had a baby son. She loved Samuel a lot. She kept the promise to God that she made to Him even before Samuel was born. God saw her great sacrifice as she gave Samuel to Eli, the temple priest, to raise. Hannah still trusted God. He blessed her with five more children.

What You Need

- ❏ this page, duplicated
- ❏ crayons
- ❏ scissors
- ❏ glue sticks
- ❏ old magazines

What to Do

1. Have the students color the cup.

2. Help the students cut out pictures from magazines of blessings such as food, clothing, books and animals.

3. Show how to glue the pictures hanging from the top rim of the cup.

4. Ask, **Does your cup overflow with blessings? You can thank God for giving you so many blessings.** Ask the students what kinds of blessings they have received from God. Explain that food, clothes, friends and even pets can be blessings.

MY

CUP

OVERFLOWS

The Lord was gracious to Hannah.
~ 1 Samuel 2:21

Hannah's Family
Finding God's Word

Memory Verse

The Lord called Samuel.
~ 1 Samuel 3:4

what to say

Hannah, Samuel's mother, took him to the temple when he was just 3 years old. Eli, the temple priest, raised Samuel to love and worship God. When Samuel was still a boy, God began to tell Samuel many things. As Samuel grew, God continued to teach Samuel important rules. Samuel listened to and obeyed God.

What You Need

❑ this page, duplicated
❑ small Bible stickers
❑ crayons

What to Do

1. Show the students how to follow the path to find letters of the alphabet. Say, **The letters will make a special word.**

2. Help the children print the letters on the path. They should also place a Bible sticker next to each letter.

3. Say, **You can find God's words in the Bible. You can tell others about God by memorizing your Bible verse each week.**

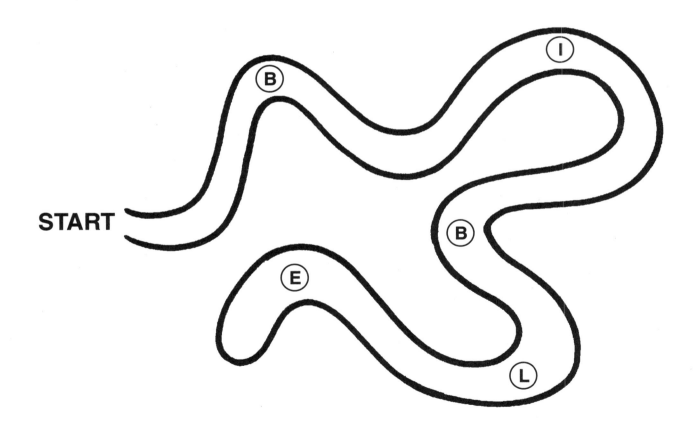

START · B · I · B · E · L

___ ___ ___ ___ ___

David's Family
With Only One Stone

Memory Verse

David said, "…Your servant will…fight him."
~ 1 Samuel 17:32

what to say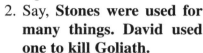

David lived in Bethlehem with his father and seven brothers. Some of David's brothers were fighting in the war against the Philistines. David's father sent him to check on his brothers. At the battle, David overheard people talking about a giant named Goliath. David wanted to fight him, but all he had was a slingshot and some stones. God was with David as he put a rock in the slingshot. He hit Goliath in the forehead and killed him.

What You Need

❑ this page, duplicated
❑ small, round brown stickers

What to Do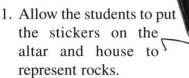

1. Allow the students to put the stickers on the altar and house to represent rocks.
2. Say, **Stones were used for many things. David used one to kill Goliath.**
3. Have the students count how many stones they used.
4. Say, **God protected David. God protects you each day and while you sleep at night.** Talk with the students about how God cares for each child, no matter how big or small they are.

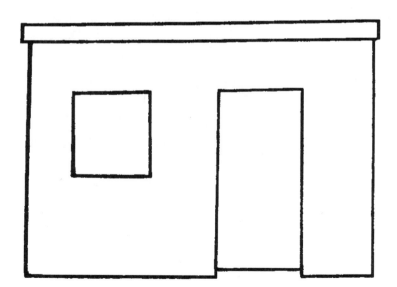

David's Family
King for a Day

Memory Verse

They anointed David king over the house of Judah.
~ 2 Samuel 2:4

what to say

The Israelites wanted a king like the other countries had. God told Samuel, the prophet, to appoint Saul as the king. At first, King Saul worshipped and obeyed God's rules. But when he began to do whatever he wanted, God got angry. Saul was no longer God's choice to be king. But Saul didn't want to stop being king. David was God's choice for the next king. King Saul died in a war against David. David became the new king.

What You Need
❑ this page, duplicated
❑ crayons

What to Do
1. Have the students color the crown.

2. Show the students how to draw a line from the crown to what a king should do to honor God.

3. Ask, **Do you think being a king is fun or hard? Why?** Talk about jobs that the children do around the house. Ask, **What would you do if you were king for a day?** Encourage the children to recognize if what they want to do honors God or does not.

59

David's Family
Training a King

Memory Verse

Solomon...shall be king.
~ 1 Kings 1:30

what to say

After David became king, he married Bathsheba. They had a son and named him Solomon. King David had other children, but he promised Bathsheba that Solomon would become the king when he died. While Solomon was growing up, King David taught him many things. Most importantly, he taught Solomon to worship and obey God. With God on their side, the king's army could fight their enemies.

What You Need

❑ this page, duplicated
❑ crayons

What to Do

1. Have the students connect the dots to reveal the most important thing Solomon would need to know (God).

2. Say, **You can know God by coming to Sunday school. You can worship God by praying and singing to Him. God is pleased when we worship Him.** Show your Bible. Tell the students that all they need to know about God is in the Bible. Say, **Although you can't read it yet, you can listen to stories and look at pictures from the Bible to know God better.**

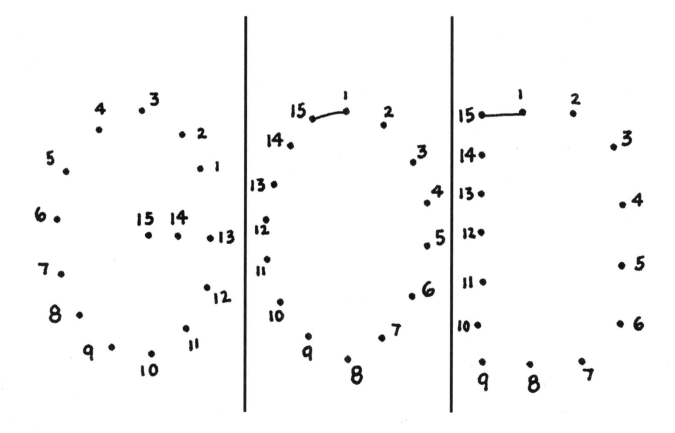

A Place to Worship God

Memory Verse

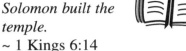

Solomon built the temple.
~ 1 Kings 6:14

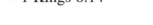 **what to say**

Before he died, King David told Solomon how to be a good king by obeying all of God's rules. In a dream, God asked Solomon what he wanted Him to do for him. Solomon knew it would take a very wise king to rule over all the Israelites, so he asked God for wisdom. King Solomon built a place of worship, called a "temple," to honor God. God was very pleased with Solomon.

What You Need

- ❏ this page, duplicated
- ❏ scissors
- ❏ glue sticks
- ❏ old magazines

What to Do

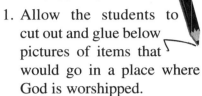

1. Allow the students to cut out and glue below pictures of items that would go in a place where God is worshipped.
2. As they work, ask them to explain their selections.
3. Say, **You can worship God anywhere! Even in your bedroom or in the car while your mom or dad is driving.** Share with them places you pray and praise God other than church.

A PLACE TO WORSHIP GOD

Esther's Family
Surprise Inside

Memory Verse

He...made her queen.
~ Esther 2:17

what to say

When Esther was young, her parents died. Her cousin Mordecai took care of her. They were Jews who worshipped only God. A king named Xerxes ruled the country. He was looking for a new queen. Many young women, including Esther, were taken to the king. Mordecai told Esther not to tell anyone she was Jewish. King Xerxes fell in love with beautiful Esther. He chose her to be his new queen.

What You Need

- ❏ this page, duplicated
- ❏ scissors
- ❏ crayons
- ❏ bright-colored stickers

What to Do

1. Have the students cut out the gift card.
2. Show how to fold the gift card to cover the heart surprise inside.
3. Allow the students to decorate the gift card.
4. Give each student a sticker to put on the bottom edge of the card to keep it closed.
5. Say, **Esther was surprised that the king loved her and made her his queen. We can also surprise people with special gifts of love. God wants us to love each other. Give this card to someone special whom you love.**

Esther's Family
Telling Others

Memory Verse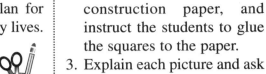

Queen Esther... reported it to the king.
~ Esther 2:22

what to say

Mordecai and Queen Esther were cousins, but no one knew that. One day, Mordecai was near the king's gate when he overheard two men making plans. They worked for the king, but they were plotting to kill him. Mordecai told Queen Esther. She told King Xerxes.

Mordecai and Esther saved the king's life. God had a plan for Queen Esther to save many lives.

What You Need

- ❑ pages 63 and 64, duplicated
- ❑ crayons
- ❑ scissors
- ❑ glue sticks
- ❑ construction paper

What to Do

1. Have the students color the pictures and then cut them out.

2. Give each student a sheet of construction paper, and instruct the students to glue the squares to the paper.

3. Explain each picture and ask the students which is their favorite way to tell someone important information. Say, **There are many ways to tell someone important information. God uses all kinds of people to do His work.**

Esther's Family
Scroll of Honor

Memory Verse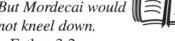

But Mordecai would not kneel down.
~ Esther 3:2

Before Class

Cut a 6" ribbon for each child.

what to say

Haman was an official to King Xerxes. Haman wanted people to kneel down and honor him. Mordecai worshipped only God. He refused to kneel down to Haman. Haman told King Xerxes some people were not obeying him. Haman asked the king for a decree to destroy all the Jews who would not bow down to him. The king said yes, but Haman and King Xerxes didn't know Queen Esther was a Jew.

What You Need

- ❏ pages 66, duplicated
- ❏ crayons
- ❏ scissors
- ❏ ribbon

What to Do

1. Have the students color and cut out the scroll.
2. Show how to roll it up and tie a ribbon around it.
3. Help the students to print their name below the phrase.
4. Say, **Scrolls were used to write decrees. A "decree" is an official order to do something very important. Your scroll says that you will honor, love and obey only God.** Ask the students to share what is important to them.

Esther's Family
Prayers for a Special Dinner

Memory Verse

I will go to the king.
~ Esther 4:16

 what to say

Haman, an official to the king, didn't like the Jews because they wouldn't bow down to him. He asked King Xerxes for a decree to kill all the Jews. Mordecai asked his cousin, Queen Esther, for help. She prayed first, then planned a special meal for the king and Haman. King Xerxes was so pleased with the meal that he told Queen Esther she could ask him for anything and he would give it to her. She asked him to save her people, the Jews.

What You Need

- ☐ this page, duplicated
- ☐ old magazines
- ☐ scissors
- ☐ glue sticks
- ☐ crayons
- ☐ 9" paper plates

What to Do

1. Have the students color and cut out the picture of Queen Esther.
2. Allow the students to cut out pictures of food from magazines and glue them to the edges of their paper plates.
3. Show how to glue the picture of Queen Esther to the center of the plate.
4. Say, **When you need help, pray to God. He will show you what to do, just like He showed Queen Esther to make a meal for the king before she asked for his favor.** Talk about how God hears our prayers and is able to help us. Give examples of your answered prayers.

I will go to the king.
~ Esther 4:16

Esther's Family
Rewards for Bravery

Memory Verse

What honor...has Mordecai received?
~ Esther 6:3

Before Class

Trace Mordecai's robe on purple paper and cut out one for each child.

 **what to say**

Mordecai helped save King Xerxes' life. He also helped his cousin Queen Esther uncover Haman's plot to kill all the Jews. Haman was an official to the king. Neither King Xerxes nor Haman knew Queen Esther was a Jew. When the king found out, he ordered Haman to be killed. To honor Mordecai, King Xerxes gave him a purple robe to wear. Mordecai also replaced Haman as an official to King Xerxes.

What You Need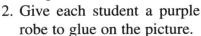

- ❑ this page, duplicated
- ❑ purple paper
- ❑ scissors
- ❑ glue sticks
- ❑ crayons

What to Do

1. Have the students color the picture of Mordecai, except for his robe.
2. Give each student a purple robe to glue on the picture.
3. Say, **You can honor God by doing what is right.** Ask them what they can do right before God, such as obeying their parents.

Jesus' Family
Gabriel the Angel

Memory Verse

"I am the Lord's servant," Mary answered.
~ Luke 1:38

Before Class

Trace the angel pattern. Use it to cut an angel from a thin sponge for each child.

 what to say

God sent Gabriel, an angel, to tell Mary something very important. Out of all the young women, God chose her to be the mother of a special baby. Gabriel told Mary she was to name the baby Jesus. Mary was both excited and afraid. Gabriel told her not to worry because God would watch over her and guide her. Mary trusted God.

What You Need

- ❑ pages 69 and 70, duplicated
- ❑ crayons
- ❑ thin sponges
- ❑ water-based paint
- ❑ paint smocks

What to Do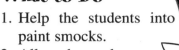

1. Help the students into paint smocks.
2. Allow the students to color the picture.
3. Give each child an angel sponge. Show how to sponge paint the angel on the picture of Mary.
4. Say, **The angel Gabriel gave good news to Mary that she would be Jesus' mother. What do you think Mary thought after Gabriel told her she would be Jesus' mother? You can tell others the good news that Jesus, the Son of God, was born!**

"I am the Lord's servant," Mary answered.
Luke 1:38

Jesus' Family
The Impossible Banner

Memory Verse

My soul glorifies the Lord.
~ Luke 1:46

what to say

Gabriel, an angel from God, told Mary she would be Jesus' mother. Gabriel also told her that her relative Elizabeth was going to have a baby. Mary thought that Elizabeth was too old to have a baby. Still, she knew that with God anything is possible. Mary went to visit Elizabeth. She found that Elizabeth was indeed going to have a baby. Mary praised God.

What You Need

- ❏ this page, duplicated
- ❏ crayons
- ❏ glue
- ❏ scissors
- ❏ large craft sticks

What to Do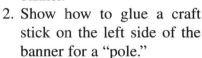

1. Allow the students to color and cut out a banner.
2. Show how to glue a craft stick on the left side of the banner for a "pole."
3. Encourage the students to take home the banner and find a special place to hang it.
4. Say, **Only God does the impossible.** Explain that praising God is like thanking Him. Ask the children for what they can praise God.

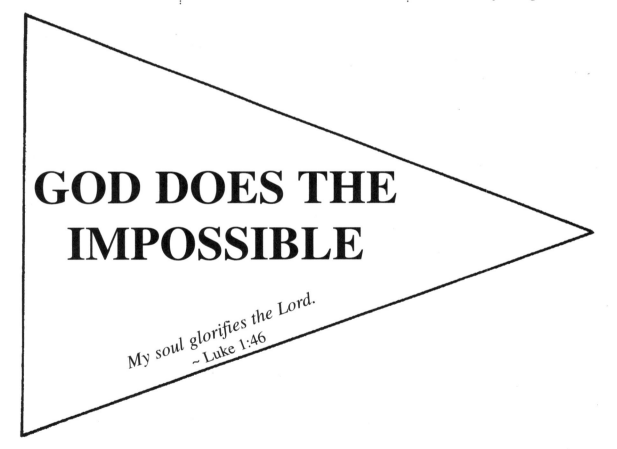

GOD DOES THE IMPOSSIBLE

My soul glorifies the Lord.
~ Luke 1:46

Jesus' Family
Is There an Angel in My Dream?

Memory Verse

An angel of the Lord appeared to him.
~ Matthew 1:20

what to say

Mary and Joseph were planning to marry. When Mary told Joseph she was going to have a baby, he decided not to marry her. He still loved her but he didn't understand that the baby she was going to have was special. An angel appeared to Joseph in a dream and told him to not be afraid. The angel said the baby Mary was going to have would be Jesus, the Son of God. Joseph then took Mary home to be his wife.

What You Need

❏ this page, duplicated
❏ crayons

What to Do

1. Have the students find and color the angel hidden in the picture.

2. Say, **God used an angel to tell Mary she was going to have baby Jesus. He used another angel to tell Joseph not to be afraid. God sends angels to watch over us. Angels are His workers.** Ask the students what they think an angel looks like. Be sure to emphasize that angels are God's helpers, but that they only do what He instructs.

Jesus' Family
Found in a Stable

Memory Verse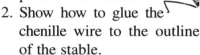

A Savior has been born to you.
~ Luke 2:11

Before Class

Cut four 3" and two 4" chenille wires for each child.

what to say

Joseph took Mary to Bethlehem. When they arrived, there was no place for them to stay. Joseph found a stable for them. Soon, Mary gave birth to baby Jesus.

In a nearby field, shepherds were taking care of their sheep. Suddenly, angels appeared in the sky. They told the shepherds a Savior had been born. The shepherds went to find the Savior. They found baby Jesus in a manger and praised God.

What You Need

- ❏ this page, duplicated
- ❏ crayons
- ❏ brown chenille wires
- ❏ large, gold star stickers
- ❏ glue

What to Do

1. Have the students color the picture of the stable.
2. Show how to glue the chenille wire to the outline of the stable.
3. Give each student a star to put above the stable.
4. Say, **Like the shepherds, you can praise God because Jesus, our Savior, was born!**

73

Jesus' Family
Sign in the Night Sky

Memory Verse

*They bowed down
and worshipped him.*
~ Matthew 2:11

Before Class

Trace (but do not cut out) the star below on gold paper for each child. On each one, write "A Savior Is Born" as shown.

God made a special star to help the wise men find Jesus. The wise men lived far away. When they saw the star, they knew the Savior had been born. They followed the star for a long time. The star hung over the house where Joseph, Mary and Jesus lived, in Bethlehem. The wise men came to worship the Savior. They gave Jesus gifts of gold, myrrh and frankincense. Then the wise men went back to their country.

What You Need

- star pattern
- glue sticks
- scissors
- gold paper
- dark blue paper

What to Do

1. Help the students cut out a gold star.
2. Allow them to glue the star on dark blue paper.
3. Say, **God gave a special star for the wise men to find the Savior. Jesus can be your Savior, too.** Ask the students where they can find Jesus today.

Jesus' Family
Different Paths

Memory Verse

*Get up...and
escape to Egypt.*
~ Matthew 2:13

what to say

King Herod told the wise men to find where Jesus lived. Herod had heard the people talking about this new "king." He didn't want Jesus to become king. When the wise men found Jesus, they gave Him their special gifts. In a dream, the wise men were warned to go back home on a different path. Then an angel appeared in a dream to Joseph and told him to take his family and go live in Egypt until it was safe to return home.

What You Need

☐ this page, duplicated
☐ crayons
☐ angel stickers

What to Do

1. Have the students trace with a crayon the path Joseph took to go to Egypt. Instruct them to place an angel sticker at the end of the safe path.

2. Say, **God used dreams to warn Joseph and the wise men to take different paths so they would be safe.** Ask the students if they come the same or different ways to church each week. Say, **Sometimes taking a new path can be fun, but we should always take the path that God tells us to take.**

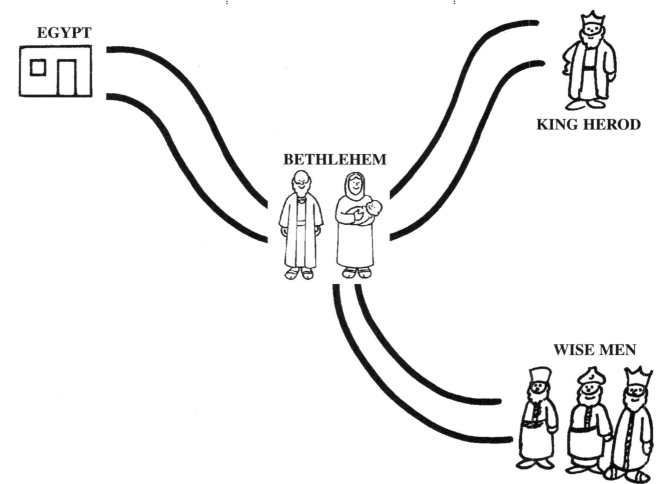

EGYPT

KING HEROD

BETHLEHEM

WISE MEN

Jesus' Family
Where to Find Jesus

Memory Verse

Jesus grew in wisdom.
~ Luke 2:52

what to say

When Jesus was 12 years old, His family went to Jerusalem to celebrate the Feast of the Passover. After the celebration ended, Joseph and Mary began to walk back home. They talked and walked with their friends and other family members. No one noticed Jesus wasn't with them until a whole day had passed! Joseph and Mary returned to Jerusalem to look for Him. When they went to the temple, they found Jesus listening and asking questions of the teachers.

What You Need

☐ this page, duplicated
☐ crayons

What to Do

1. Instruct the students to color each square that has a number in it. They should not color any squares that have letters in them.
2. Have the students write the letters they find on the lines below the square.
3. Ask the children if they have a favorite Bible story. Talk about how the students can know more about Jesus by listening to Bible stories.

6	8	I	7	3	2
B	3	2	5	8	1
9	1	8	4	L	4
3	2	7	3	2	1
1	3	9	B	3	7
7	4	5	8	2	E

_____   _____   _____   _____

Jesus' Family
Blind But Now I See

Memory Verse

Neither this man nor his parents sinned.
~ John 9:3

what to say

Mary and Joseph raised Jesus to love God and work for Him. After Jesus grew up, He walked from town to town. Sometimes He spoke to large crowds. He saw blind, crippled and sick people. People heard that Jesus could heal them. One man Jesus met was blind. Some teachers asked Jesus if the man or his parents had sinned and caused the blindness. Jesus said that no one had sinned. Jesus put mud on the man's eyes. When the man washed away the mud, he could see. It was a miracle from God to help the people believe in Him.

What You Need

❏ this page, duplicated
❏ crayons

What to Do

1. Have the students color the picture of the blind man that Jesus healed.
2. Say, **Close your eyes and pretend you can't see, then open them. It was a miracle that Jesus made the man see again. Jesus loves and cares about everyone. He loves and cares about you.** Explain that only God or Jesus can perform a miracle.

Zechariah's Family
Praising Hands

Memory Verse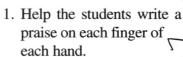

You will be silent.
~ Luke 1:20

what to say

Zechariah was a priest at the temple. Zechariah and Elizabeth prayed for children, but they had not had one. Now Elizabeth was too old. One day when Zechariah went to the temple, he saw the angel Gabriel. Gabriel told Zechariah that Elizabeth would have a special baby. Zechariah didn't believe him, so Gabriel told him he wouldn't be able to speak until the baby was born. Zechariah wasn't able to speak until his son, John, was born. God had big plans for John.

What You Need

- [ ] this page, duplicated
- [ ] pencils
- [ ] crayons

What to Do

1. Help the students write a praise on each finger of each hand.
2. Allow the students to lightly color the hands.
3. Say, **Praising God is another way of saying "thank You" to God.** Ask the students why we need to praise God. Ask what they have thanked God for this week. Share with the children how you praise God.

Zechariah's Family
Trumpet Announcement

Memory Verse

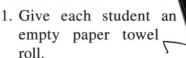

His name is John.
~ Luke 1:63

Before Class

Cut two ½" x 6" pieces of ribbon for each child.

what to say

Zechariah and Elizabeth had been married many years but they had no children. Elizabeth was old when an angel told Zechariah his wife would have a son. They were to name him "John." Elizabeth gave birth to a boy. She knew she was to name him John, but it was the custom to name the first son after the father. Zechariah and Elizabeth obeyed God and named their son John, as the angel had told them. John would be a special worker for God.

What You Need

- [ ] page 80, duplicated
- [ ] paper towel rolls
- [ ] crayons
- [ ] glue
- [ ] scissors
- [ ] ribbon

What to Do

1. Give each student an empty paper towel roll.
2. Allow the students to color and cut out the trumpet cover.
3. Show how to put glue on the paper towel roll and wrap the trumpet cover on it.
4. Instruct the students to glue a ribbon around each end of the trumpet.
5. Tell the students that they can use the trumpet to announce the good news that Elizabeth gave birth to a boy and they named him John. Say, **The Bible says that John was born to prepare people for Jesus.**

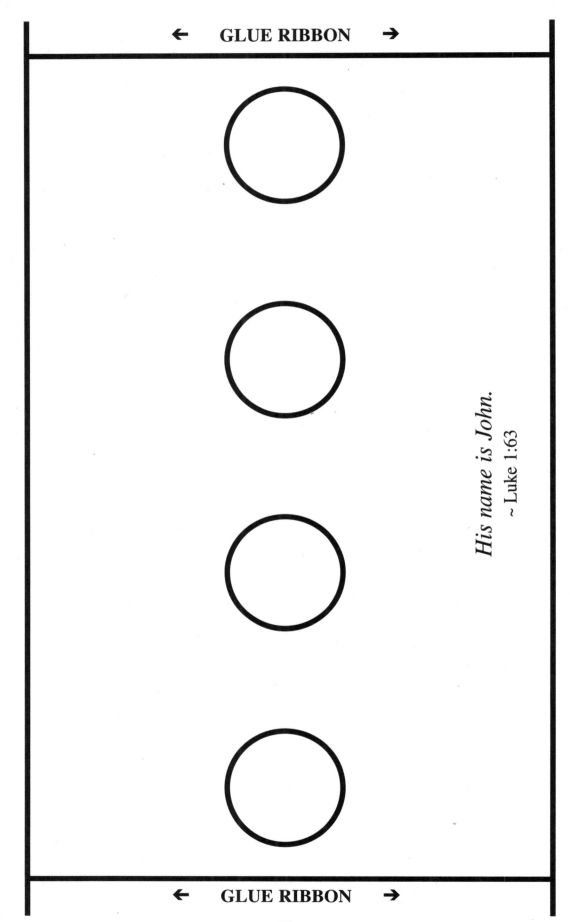

Zechariah's Family
Paper Sandals

Memory Verse

Jesus was baptized.
~ Matthew 3:16

Before Class

Use the pattern to cut two straps for each child.

After John the Baptist grew up, he wore clothes made from camel's hair. He ate honey and locusts and he lived in the desert. John began to prepare the people for Jesus. He told them they needed to be sorry for their sins and get baptized. One day, Jesus asked John to baptize Him. John didn't feel worthy to even carry Jesus' sandals, but he did as Jesus asked. God was pleased. Zechariah and Elizabeth's son helped God with His plan.

What You Need

- ❏ this page, duplicated
- ❏ scissors
- ❏ stapler
- ❏ brown paper bags
- ❏ tape

What to Do

1. Trace around each child's shoes on brown bags and cut them out. Make the tracings larger than their actual shoes.

2. Give each child two straps.

3. Help the children staple a strap across the toe area of each sandal. Place clear tape over the staples to avoid injury.

4. Show the students how they can carefully slide their shoes into the sandals. Encourage them to walk slowly because the sandals might be slippery.

5. Say, **John didn't feel worthy to carry Jesus' sandals. Yet we were so important to Jesus that He ended up dying on a cross for our sins. As you walk in your sandals, remember: you are special to Jesus!**

Zechariah's Family
Chained to Truth

Memory Verse

Herod feared John and protected him.
~ Mark 6:20

Before Class

Cut several 6" x 1" strips from black paper for each child.

what to say

John the Baptist came to prepare the people for Jesus. The people had sin in their lives. He told them they needed to be sorry. After they said they were sorry, John baptized them. John told King Herod that it was against the law for him to be married to his brother's wife. The king didn't like what John said, so he put him in jail. Even so, the king was afraid of John because he knew he was a holy man who preached about Jesus.

What You Need

- ❏ this page, duplicated
- ❏ black paper
- ❏ scissors
- ❏ glue sticks
- ❏ white crayons

What to Do

1. Write or have the students write the memory verse on a black strip.
2. Show how to glue more plain strips together with that one to form a long chain.
2. Say, **Even though John was in jail and his feet and hands were in chains, he still spoke the truth to anyone who would listen. You can freely tell others about Jesus. Talk about how Christians in other countries aren't supposed to talk about Jesus.**

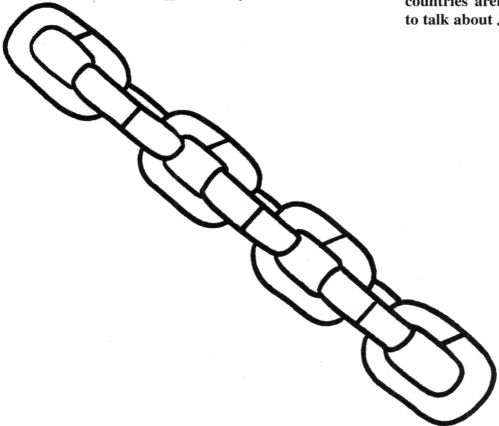

Mary, Martha and Lazarus
A Good Place to Listen

Memory Verse

Mary...sat at the Lord's feet.
~ Luke 10:39

what to say

Jesus walked around the countryside with His disciples. One day, Jesus saw His friends Mary and Martha, who were sisters. They invited Jesus and the disciples to eat dinner with them. While Martha was busy preparing dinner, Mary sat and listened to Jesus. Martha became angry. She asked Jesus to tell Mary to help her. Instead, Jesus told Martha that Mary was right to be still and listen to Him.

What You Need

- ❑ this page, duplicated
- ❑ crayons
- ❑ scissors
- ❑ glue sticks
- ❑ large construction paper
- ❑ clear, self-stick plastic

What to Do

1. Have the students color and cut out the pictures and glue them on a sheet of construction paper.

2. Go around and write the memory verse on each sheet, then cover the sheet with clear plastic.

3. Say, **Mary sat at Jesus' feet and listened to Him. You can sit on your mat while you listen to your teachers talk about Jesus in Sunday school.** After the mats are completed, encourage the students to sit on them while you share the Bible story.

Mary, Martha and Lazarus
Lazarus Is Alive

Memory Verse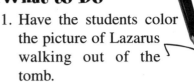

It is for God's glory.
~ John 11:4

Before Class

Trace and cut out a rock for each child. Punch a hole in each rock and at the corresponding spot on each coloring sheet.

what to say

Mary, Martha and Lazarus were brother and sisters. They were also Jesus' friends. When Lazarus became very sick, Mary and Martha asked Jesus to come quickly. They knew He had the power to heal people.

But Jesus stayed where He was for two more days. Lazarus died! When Jesus arrived at their house, everyone was sad. Jesus told Martha that Lazarus would be alive again. He went to the tomb where Lazarus was buried and said, "Lazarus, come out." Lazarus walked out of the tomb. He was alive!

What You Need

- ❑ pages 84 and 85, duplicated
- ❑ crayons
- ❑ scissors
- ❑ hole punch
- ❑ tape
- ❑ paper fasteners

What to Do

1. Have the students color the picture of Lazarus walking out of the tomb.
2. Give each child a rock to color.
3. Help the students fit a paper fastener through the hole in the rock and the hole in the picture. Open the fastener so it holds the rock and place tape across the back of the fastener.
4. Show how to roll away the rock to show Lazarus alive.

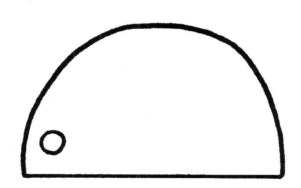

It is for God's glory.
John 11:4

Mary, Martha and Lazarus
How to Honor Jesus

Memory Verse

She poured it on Jesus' feet.
~ John 12:3

Before Class

Cut poster board into one 4" x 4" square for each child.

what to say

Martha prepared a special meal for Jesus. She remembered Jesus had raised her brother from the dead. Her sister Mary also wanted to do something special for Jesus. She had an expensive jar of perfume. It cost as much as a whole year's worth of wages! Without saying a word, she poured it on Jesus' feet and wiped His feet dry with her long hair. This was Mary's way of showing honor to Jesus.

What You Need

- ❏ this page, duplicated
- ❏ crayons
- ❏ scissors
- ❏ poster board
- ❏ glue sticks

What to Do

1. Allow the students to color the table tent.
2. Have them cut it out and glue it to a poster board square.
3. When the tents are dry, fold them in half at the dashed line so they stand up like tents.
4. Say, **You can put your table tent on your table at home. Martha and Mary honored Jesus. You can honor Him by saying a prayer before you eat. Your table tent will remind you to pray.** Tell the students what you say when you pray before a meal.

She poured it on Jesus' feet.
~ John 12:3

I HONOR
JESUS WITH
MY PRAYERS

A Father and Two Sons
Foolish or Wise Bank

Memory Verse

Father, I have sinned.
~ Luke 15:18

Before Class

Trace a penny on gold paper and cut out several for each child.

what to say

Once there was a man who had two sons. The youngest son asked for his inheritance money. His father gave it to him. The youngest son went to another town to live. There, he spent all his money having a good time. Then he decided to go home and ask his father to forgive him. The youngest son had figured out that it would have been more wise to save his money instead of spending it foolishly. His father was happy to see him.

What You Need

- [ ] this page, duplicated
- [ ] penny
- [ ] gold paper
- [ ] scissors
- [ ] glue sticks

What to Do

1. Read the title of each bank to the children.
2. Instruct the students to glue some paper coins on the bank they think is the right one.
3. Say, **It is wiser to save money than to spend it on foolish things. You can learn to save your money by putting it in your bank at home. God wants us to be careful with our money.**

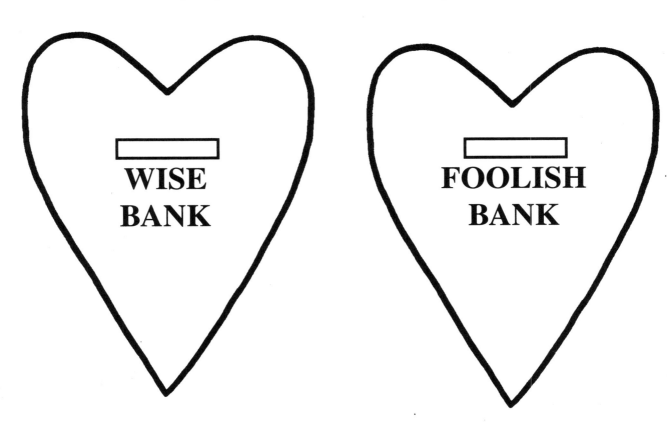

WISE BANK

FOOLISH BANK

A Father and Two Sons
Decision Maze

Memory Verse

The older brother became angry.
~ Luke 15:28

what to say

A father gave his youngest son his inheritance money when he asked for it. The young son spent it foolishly. When he returned home, the young son asked to be forgiven. His father was so happy to see him that he gave him new clothes, a ring and even a party! When the older son found out, he was mad. He didn't understand why his father would give the young son a party for being foolish. He refused to go to the party.

What You Need

- ❑ this page, duplicated
- ❑ crayons

What to Do

1. Have the students draw a line to show the path the older brother decided to take.

2. Then using a different crayon, they should draw a line to the party.

3. Say, **The older brother chose the path that leads to anger and jealousy. His father was happy that his younger son had become wise. You can make wise decisions.** Ask the students to describe what it means to be wise.

A Father and Two Sons
Lost and Found Son

Bible Story
The father shares his wisdom.
(Luke 15:11-32)

Memory Verse

We had to celebrate and be glad.
~ Luke 15:32

Before Class

For each child, poke a hole in a paper plate with the point of your scissors.

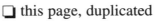
what to say

Because the father was wise, he let his youngest son lose himself in the ways of the world. The young son spent all of his money on foolish things. Soon, the youngest son became wise and returned home. The older son was so full of anger, he couldn't understand why his father was happy. The father was happy because his youngest son had been lost and now he was found.

What You Need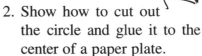

- this page, duplicated
- crayons
- scissors
- glue sticks
- paper fasteners
- tape
- 6" paper plates

What to Do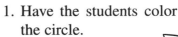

1. Have the students color the circle.
2. Show how to cut out the circle and glue it to the center of a paper plate.
3. Instruct the students to cut out the half circle.
4. Go around and poke a paper fastener through the half circle and the paper plate. Place a strip of tape on the back of the paper fastener to avoid injury.
5. Show how to cover up the lost son or the found son. Ask, **Which will you choose to be: wise or foolish?**

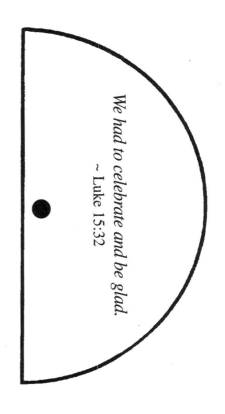

89

Family of God
Sin Makes Me Sad

Memory Verse

All have sinned.
~ Romans 3:23

what to say

Ever since Adam and Eve sinned in the garden, we are all born sinners. Adam and Eve disobeyed God. Sin means disobeying God by doing bad things, like telling a lie or hitting. Sin makes God sad. God loves us so much that He is waiting for us to tell Him that we are sinners. He will forgive us when we sin, but we must ask for His forgiveness.

What You Need

❏ this page, duplicated
❏ crayons

What to Do

1. Have the students draw a line from SIN to each picture that shows someone sinning.

2. Instruct them to draw a sad face beside each picture that shows sinning.

3. Say, **God is sad when you sin. Explain that both adults and children sin.** Share some of the sins adults can do, like getting angry and saying bad words. Ask the students how they feel when they sin.

90

Family of God
He Took My Punishment

Bible Story
Christ died on the cross for our sins. (Romans 5:6-8)

Memory Verse

Christ died for us.
~ Romans 5:8

what to say

Have you ever done something bad and got caught by your parents? What if a friend said that she would take your punishment for you? How would you feel? That is what Christ did for all of us when He died on the cross. Christ, or Jesus as you may know Him, never did anything bad. He never sinned. Sins keep us from going to heaven. Christ took your punishment for your sins.

What You Need

- [ ] this page, duplicated
- [ ] crayons

What to Do

1. Instruct the students to connect the broken lines on the cross to spell MY SINS.

2. Say, **Jesus paid the price for your sins when He died on the cross.** This is a difficult concept for children to understand. Be sure to explain that even good children sin. Emphasize that God loves them!

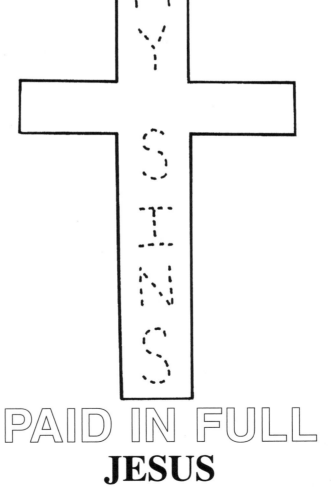

PAID IN FULL
JESUS

91

Family of God
Letter to God

Memory Verse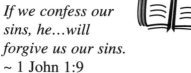

If we confess our sins, he...will forgive us our sins.
~ 1 John 1:9

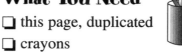 what to say

God loves us and wants us all to live in heaven with Him forever! Sin keeps us from going to heaven. Sin is doing something bad like hitting or telling a lie. God sees our sins. He wants us to tell Him our sins and ask Him to forgive us. God freely forgives us when we ask Him because He loves us.

What You Need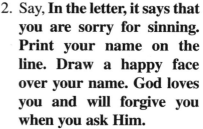

❑ this page, duplicated
❑ crayons

What to Do

1. Give each student a copy of the letter.

2. Say, **In the letter, it says that you are sorry for sinning. Print your name on the line. Draw a happy face over your name. God loves you and will forgive you when you ask Him.**

3. As you help the students print their names, explain how much God loves them and wants to forgive them. Emphasize that they are good children who sometimes do bad things.

Dear God,

I am sorry for sinning.

_____
Name

Family of God
Jesus, My Savior

Memory Verse

Whoever believes in him shall...have eternal life.
~ John 3:16

what to say

God loves us so much, He wants all of us to live in heaven with Him forever! Jesus took the punishment for our sins when He died on the cross. The Bible says that if we tell God that we are sinners, ask Him to forgive us and understand that Jesus died for our sins, we can live in heaven forever!

What You Need

- ❏ page 94, duplicated
- ❏ water-based paint
- ❏ paintbrushes
- ❏ paint smocks

What to Do

1. Help the children into paint smocks.
2. Allow the students to paint the picture of Jesus.
3. Say, **Jesus loves you so much. You can be part of God's family when you ask Jesus to come into your heart.** Salvation is a difficult concept for children. Ask them if they have any questions about it.

JESUS IS MY SAVIOR!

Whoever believes in him shall...have eternal life.
John 3:16